CountryLiving

TINY HOMES

CountryLiving
TINY HOMES

Living Big in Small Spaces

Edited by Caroline McKenzie

HEARST
books

CONTENTS

Maine Attraction

1,200
square feet

SOUTHWEST HARBOR,
MAINE

Logged In

1,200
square feet

VASHON ISLAND,
WASHINGTON

Finders Keepers

1,200
square feet

MCKINNEY,
TEXAS

Open Season

1,200
square feet

AUSTIN,
TEXAS

20

The Minimalist Escape

1,456
square feet

PENDLETON,
INDIANA

28

Sunny-Side Up

1,375
square feet

SARASOTA,
FLORIDA

36

Out of the Blue

1,325
square feet

SPRUCE GROVE,
ALBERTA, CANADA

42

Neutral Territory

1,200
square feet

RHINEBECK,
NEW YORK

76

Ranch Reform

1,145
square feet

VENTURA COUNTY,
CALIFORNIA

82

Hillside Hideaway

1,100
square feet

BUCKS COUNTY,
PENNSYLVANIA

86

Country Strong

1,000
square feet

ACADIA,
OKLAHOMA

92

Calm, Cool, and Collected

1,000
square feet

SHARON,
CONNECTICUT

In Bloom

970
square feet

REDLANDS,
CALIFORNIA

Shipshape Stunner

880
square feet

NANTUCKET,
MASSACHUSETTS

Charm School

858
square feet

HOBART,
NEW YORK

One-Kit Wonder

800
square feet

NAPA,
CALIFORNIA

Garden Variety

600
square feet

DOUGLAS,
GEORGIA

Open-House Policy

500
square feet

ELKINS,
NEW HAMPSHIRE

Work of Art

480
square feet

HARPERSVILLE,
ALABAMA

Shedding Style

250
square feet

DALLAS,
TEXAS

128

City Savvy

735
square feet

NEW YORK,
NEW YORK

134

Lofty Aspirations

700
square feet

MINNEAPOLIS,
MINNESOTA

140

Forest Station

665
square feet

DAYTON,
WYOMING

144

Party On

600
square feet

WILMINGTON,
DELAWARE

172

Southern Comforts

192
square feet

NATCHEZ,
MISSISSIPPI

176

Small Wonder

192
square feet

PORTLAND,
OREGON

184

Happy Little Camper

100
square feet

ST. GEORGE,
UTAH

190

Room with a View

100
square feet

NASHVILLE,
TENNESSEE

INTRODUCTION

It may seem counterintuitive for a magazine that regularly showcases sprawling farmhouses and wide-open acreage to become an authority on all things small. But in the past few years at *Country Living*, we've witnessed a seemingly insatiable hunger for small spaces of all sorts—from charming she-sheds to happy campers to quaint little cottages.

While on its surface the Tiny House Movement may seem contradictory to pastoral life, it's actually rooted in something inherently country: simplicity. The "call of small" speaks to those seeking to pare down—to focus less on minutiae and more on what matters—and that, in a nutshell, is the heart and soul of *Country Living*, no matter your square footage.

Throughout these pages, you'll find seemingly boundless, outside-the-box inspiration for living well with less, whether it's a whimsical treehouse designed for whiling away an afternoon (190) or an unbelievably chic garden shed equipped for both roses and rosé (152). These small wonders prove that compact living doesn't have to come at the cost of character, nor does it demand a minimalist approach to decorating. In fact, many of the hallmarks of country design—an aesthetic that's essentially rooted in the idea of living resourcefully, after all—are right at home

in small spaces. Easy-access open shelving, sliding barn doors, flush-mount schoolhouse lighting, and bench seating at the farm table are all beautiful and practical choices when there's hardly a square foot to spare. Functional collectibles such as mason jars serve double-duty as decoration and storage. Even our affection for linear motifs—ticking stripes on linens, beadboard paneling on walls—proves useful when it comes to making a space feel larger.

So whether you're looking to carve out your own backyard escape (169 or 172), trying to infuse a tiny city apartment with country charm (128), or simply looking to downsize, take big inspiration from those who've made the (tiny!) leap. They know that a little room to breathe is really the only room you need.

Rachel Hardage Barrett
Editor-in-Chief, *Country Living*

Part One

The
SMALL
of
FAME

20

BIGGER AND
BETTER IDEAS

|*No.* 1| *Peg Rail*

Peg rails originated in the living spaces of the Shaker community. The handcrafted railing often bordered an entire room at shoulder level for easy storage of chairs, baskets, and the like. Today it's a stylish, streamlined way to wrangle clutter in foyers, mudrooms, or hallways.

| *№.* **2** | *Barn Doors*

Whether used on cabinetry, as shown here, or between adjoining rooms, this country icon isn't just super charming; it's also super functional. Why? Tract-hinged doors don't require the wide radius of their traditional counterparts, making them ideal for tight spaces or narrow hallways. Use a salvaged door or coat a new one with chalkboard paint to make an even smarter statement.

| *№.* **3** | *Wall-Mounted Desks*

Make your walls work overtime with a wall-mounted desk, which can fold up when not in use. The versatile piece also easily transitions into a cocktail bar, a craft station, or, if you equip it with a mirror, a vanity.

| №·4 | *Retro Appliances*

Generally speaking, vintage and vintage-inspired appliances such as Big Chill® and SMEG® have a smaller footprint than modern-day behemoths. They also add decorative panache—and a welcome pop of color!—in a small space.

| №·5 | *Built-In Beds*

Tucking beds into alcoves and otherwise unused wall recesses instantly increases the available floor space in a room. (And talk about a sweet spot to snooze!) To double down on efficiency, consider incorporating bunk beds where ceiling height allows.

To-Dos

☐ Plan date night

☐ Call Mom

☐ Farmers' market

☑ Post Office

| №·6 | *Converted Closets*

How do you add a new room to a tiny house without a full-blown renovation? Reimagine a closet! Whether you carve out a home office, a craft room, a bar, or even a guestroom with a foldaway bed, you can amp up a house's living space with smart furnishings and a splash of color. (The latter will help differentiate the area from its surroundings.)

| №·7 | *Folding Chairs*

Handsome wood folding chairs are attractive enough to garner a spot around a formal dining table. But their real beauty lies in their storability. The collapsible perches can be cleared at a moment's notice, letting a small house's eating area quickly transition to another use.

| №·8 | *Mirrors*

Trick the eye into seeing a bigger room with the introduction of mirrors. The light-reflecting surfaces amp up the natural light and surrounding views. Go all in with a single oversize one, or try a floor-to-ceiling assortment like the ones lining the walls of this sunny bathroom.

| № · 9 | *Sconces*

Nightstands are a luxury in a tiny home. If you're lucky enough to squeeze one (or better, yet, two!) into your sleeping quarters, you'll want to maximize them by replacing table lamps with wall-mounted sconces. Electric or hardwired, the fixtures will illuminate a bedside without encroaching on precious real estate.

| № · 10 | *Coffee Table Trunks*

Don't squander precious floor space with a coffee table that fails to earn its keep. Instead use an old trunk for this living room essential. You'll infuse the space with storied style and also handily conceal throw blankets, computer chargers, kids' toys, and more.

| №·11 | *Open Shelving*

In kitchens, bathrooms, and just about anywhere else, you can take the strain off a cramped room by swapping bulky cabinets with airy open shelves. The streamlined storage transforms utilitarian pieces into works of art and also alleviates the awkward angles that can arise from squeezed-in cabinet doors.

| №·12 | *Elevated Draperies*

The easiest way to make a room feel taller is to place the curtain rod *really* close to the ceiling—roughly two inches from the crown molding. While you're at it, extend the rod four inches on either side of the window so it appears wider and lets in more light.

|№·13| *Rolling Furniture*

Small spaces need to be quick-change artists, which is why everything is better on wheels. From coffee tables and bar carts to beds and dining tables, caster-adorned furniture lets you change up a room's functionality with ease.

| No. 14 | *Reclaimed Storage*

Repurposed crates, bins, and boxes add heaps of charm to any home but are especially well-placed in a tiny one, where they can do double duty as décor and as a means of stashing supplies.

| No. 15 | *Skirted Pieces*

What do console tables, bathroom sinks, and kitchen cabinets have in common? They all look better sporting a skirt. Fabric-covered pieces introduce some feminine flair to a space and sub in visual interest in place of too-big-for-a-tiny-home architectural elements. They're also easier to access in a tight space.

| *№·* **16** | *Barely-there Shades*

When in doubt, get it in white. While color can work wonders in a tiny home, a neutral palette is a foolproof plan for creating a more open feel. Coat walls, ceilings, and even floors in creamy white paint, and then layer in warm tones with touches of wood and brass.

|№.17| *Acrylic Accents*

This crystal-clear, plastic-like material will streamline a small room by eliminating visual clutter. And don't stop at barstools: Acrylic coffee tables, consoles, trays, and drawer pulls have the same effect.

Bring ladylike curves
to a compact space.

| *№.* **18** | *Settees*

Yes, a full-size sofa can work in a space-challenged house, but some rooms call for something less intrusive. Enter settees, which can comfortably seat two people and have a small footprint to boot.

| *№.* **19** | *Under-the-Eaves Spaces*

A set-in-the-rafters room is hands-down the hardest working area in a tiny home. A common place for a sleeping loft, they also make cozy offices and playrooms. If your home's floorplan doesn't allow for a set of stairs, try accessing by ladder.

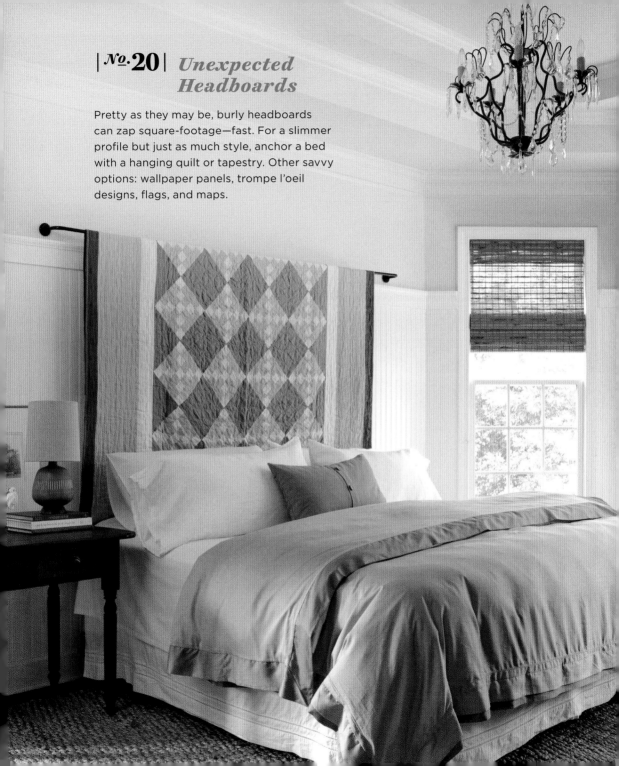

| No. 20 | *Unexpected Headboards*

Pretty as they may be, burly headboards can zap square-footage—fast. For a slimmer profile but just as much style, anchor a bed with a hanging quilt or tapestry. Other savvy options: wallpaper panels, trompe l'oeil designs, flags, and maps.

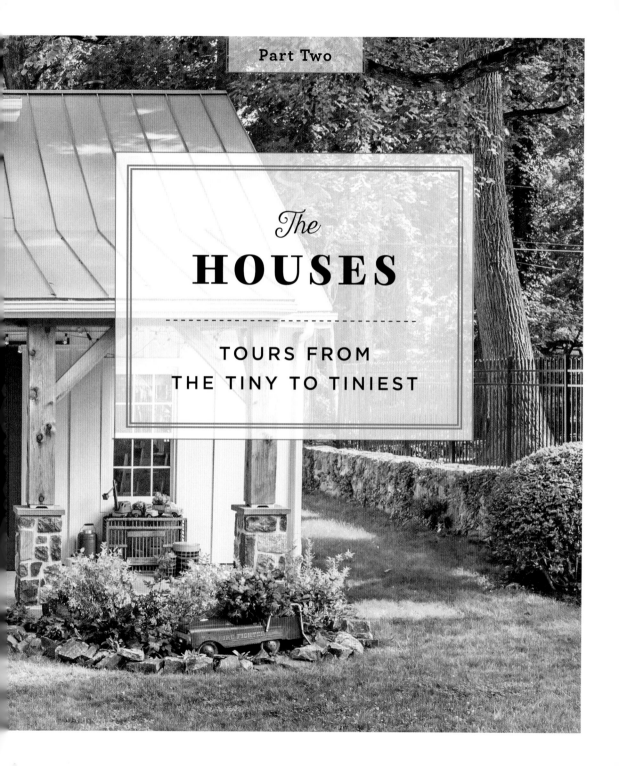

Part Two

The

HOUSES

TOURS FROM
THE TINY TO TINIEST

The Minimalist Escape

This new-construction farmhouse sits on seven acres and comprises 728 square feet of living space and a garage of the same size. (The homeowners added the latter to their house plan so it would meet the county's minimum size requirement of 1,400 square feet.) Inside the home, there's a nearly-all-white palette and an airy, less-is-more aesthetic.

◄ In an effort to utilize every nook and cranny, the homeowners turned an unused area under the staircase into a doghouse alcove. The same ingenuity was applied to craft a slim bookcase to the right. The colorful collections of cookbooks and paperbacks bring a bright pop to the neutral surroundings.

▼ Minimal kitchen storage calls for creativity. In this case, everyday kitchen items are stored in the living room; a chippy old bookcase transforms dishes and enamel cookware into a would-be art installation. Given the home's size and open floor plan, the living room placement is a mere arm's reach from the kitchen.

◄ The wood stove adds character and, thanks to the house's size, also provides plenty of warmth during frigid Midwest winters. It sits atop porcelain tiles that mimic the look of hardwood floors but are more heat-resistant than the surrounding planked floors. The tiles' dark "stain" also lends a visual anchor.

► Simplicity reigns in the kitchen, where modern pieces like the flat-fronted cabinetry, a sleek range, and plug-in pendant lights mix with more rustic items, including the raw-wood open shelving and homemade bar stools. The star is an antique pine table. Outfitted with casters, this portable island can be repositioned as needed.

A sliding barn door brings character while eating up less floor space than a traditional door. This one was crafted from a cast-off section of beadboard paneling. Beyond the door, a black claw-foot tub makes a statement in the house's only bathroom.

The homeowners salvaged the door from a local tobacco barn and then cut it down to size.

Prefabricated vanities won't always squeeze into a compact bathroom. Enter this do-it-yourself model that features metal pipe legs topped with an old door. Low-cost mirrors and simple Edison-bulb light fixtures complete the room.

The farmhouse's clean, crisp palette extends to the bedroom—from hard materials like the white walls and pine railings to softer elements such as the blue-and-white subtly striped bedding, textured pillows, and simple duvet cover.

When room inside is limited, look to the outdoors. Here, a cast-iron sink becomes a makeshift mudroom where the homeowners can kick off boots, hang hats, and tend to container gardens brimming with herbs and vegetables.

1 **Give big-box furniture a try.**
On the hunt for a tiny house sofa? Check out retailers such as Target® and IKEA® for offerings that are high in style but small in size. This neutral slipcovered sofa came from Ikea and perfectly nestles up to the narrow coffee table.

2 **Incorporate wood tones.**
A neutral space still needs warmth. The homeowners achieved that effect with a wealth of wooden finishes, including the raw pine railings, oak side chair, and mahogany front door. The rough-hewn accents also connect to the sprawling acreage outside.

3 **Skip window treatments.**
With no neighbors in sight, privacy becomes a moot point. Going bare on the windows maximizes natural light and keeps a room from feeling weighed down by the visual heft of voluminous curtains.

BIG IDEAS

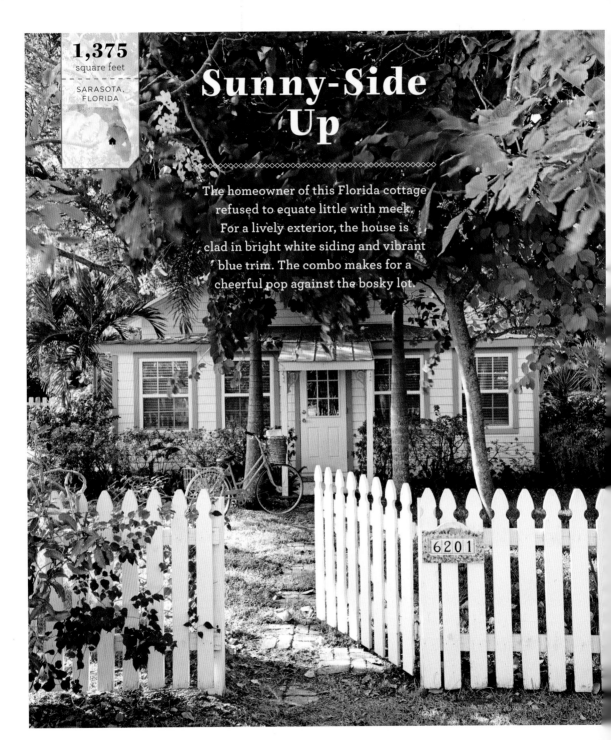

1,375
square feet

SARASOTA,
FLORIDA

Sunny-Side Up

The homeowner of this Florida cottage
refused to equate little with meek.
For a lively exterior, the house is
clad in bright white siding and vibrant
blue trim. The combo makes for a
cheerful pop against the bosky lot.

6201

Architectural flourishes give a tiny cottage big character. Here, louvered shutters and a thrift-store ledge, both painted to match the home's cheery blue trim, transform the thirteen-inch-wide window into an exterior focal point.

➤ The cottage's breakfast nook is chock-full of hardworking pieces. The backless bench offers equal seating to a host of chairs and can be tucked under the table when not in use. (And it doesn't block the view of the handsome butler's pantry.) Similarly, the rough-hewn farm table utilizes every last inch—the pullout drawer houses cutlery, and slots carved into the end are a sweet spot to stash wooden spoons.

◄ One way to maximize efficiency in a cramped kitchen is to assign each area a specific task. The homeowner transformed this otherwise unused corner into a coffee station, with two narrow shelves holding mugs and canisters. Below, a pink-topped marble buffet conceals a coffee pot and microwave.

The low-pitched ceilings made a standard-height shower impossible but could still accommodate a restored cast-iron tub. Above it, a yard of cheesecloth is strewn from Shaker pegs to lend privacy without blocking the window's natural light.

◄ The homeowner incorporated guest quarters by positioning a twin bed directly against a wall in the study. The green chalkboard provides a space-saving, statement-making headboard.

◄ The master bedroom's various posts and beams present furniture-arranging challenges. The unconventional placement of the blue antique sleeper in front of not one window but two produces a cozy nook. It also frees up walls for other storage pieces.

⋀ Sometimes a big sofa is just right. That's the case with this nine-foot-long antique one. The oversize item visually anchors the room and provides ample seating in one fell swoop. Covered in durable, affordable paint drop cloths, the neutral piece artfully blends with its surroundings, making it feel well suited, not overpowering.

▲ One way to create additional space: Take it to the rafters. Vaulted ceilings increase the room's height by four feet. That uptick helps the home office feel airy in spite of its modest footprint. Down below, the antique rug brings warm tones to the white room.

1 **Start with a neutral backdrop.** Creamy white walls and whitewashed plywood floors allow the kitchen to feel more expansive.

2 **Stay on track.** Large light fixtures over an island bring a wow factor. They also bring some serious heft. Track lighting, seamlessly run along the kitchen's exposed beams, illuminates the room and takes up very little space. A petite pendant over the sink—an architectural salvage find— recoups some of the sculptural panache.

3 **Pull up a barstool.** Even in a kitchen like this one, which doesn't have a bar with an overhang for stools, barstools are a game-changer. Let them serve as a counter-side seat and a place to rest groceries, tote bags, and more.

The plywood was thousands of dollars cheaper than staining hardwood flooring.

1,325
square feet

SPRUCE GROVE,
ALBERTA, CANADA

Out of
the Blue

The homeowners swapped square
footage for wide-open spaces when they
relocated from a sprawling city home
to a quaint white farmhouse situated
on twenty acres in Alberta, Canada.

◄ No playroom? No problem! In lieu of a full-blown rec room, a pint-size antique desk serves as a craft and reading area. A storage compartment below the desktop makes it an efficient accent piece. Meanwhile, the room's blue-washed paneling is a colorful contrast to the warm wood tones of the desk and oversize dresser.

◄ The 1940s farmhouse came with no closets at all. The homeowners added his-and-hers closets to two corners of the master bedroom and then outfitted the space between with a built-in tabletop surface. (This works as a desk, as well as a vanity.) Adding to the storage is a pair of dressers on either side of the bed, which serve as nightstands and also conceal off-season clothing.

► The homeowner opted for a table that best suits a family of four (as opposed to a larger one to accommodate occasional guests.) A single chair in bright blue introduces a pop of color and visually connects to the adjoining blue-and-white living room. Similarly, extending subway tile from the kitchen to the dining area makes the two tight spaces feel like one larger room.

1 Say it with an accent. To help tight quarters feel more cohesive, use one accent throughout the home. Here, crisp white paint on the walls and ceilings and light pine floors establish a neutral base, while blue draperies complement the large stretch of sky outside the windows.

2 Turn the front door into artwork. When walls are limited, a splash of color on an exterior or interior door can be a savvy substitute. The home's dusty-blue front door brings a colorful, sculptural element to the room, much as a piece of art would.

3 Pick furniture with flexibility. Look closely: Four of the living room's five seating options are easy to pick up and shift around. Portable pieces like these rockers and X-benches let a small living room quickly transition into a party space, play area, and more.

BIG IDEAS

MOUNTAIN VIEW

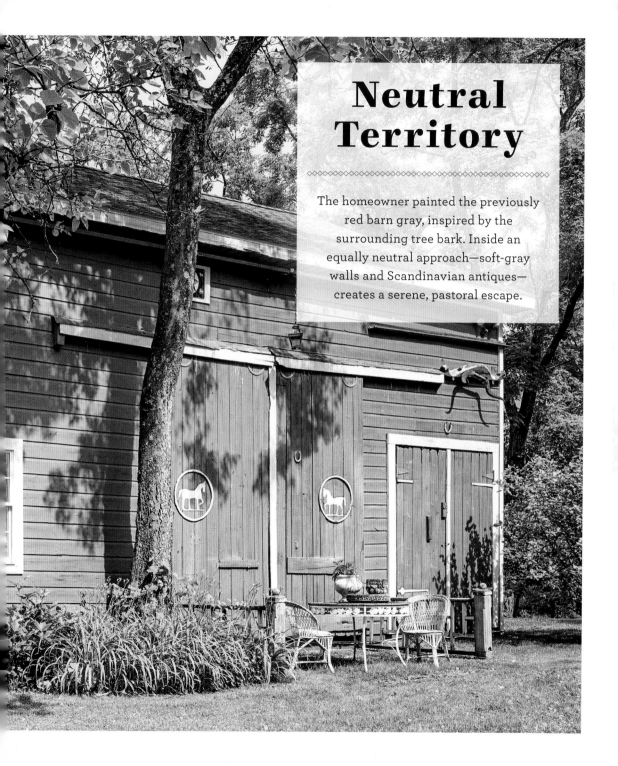

Neutral Territory

The homeowner painted the previously red barn gray, inspired by the surrounding tree bark. Inside an equally neutral approach—soft-gray walls and Scandinavian antiques— creates a serene, pastoral escape.

Paint the floors the
same neutral shade
as the walls to up the
open-and-airy factor.

Kitchens can overpower a tiny, open floor plan. Keeping that dominance at bay is a less-is-more aesthetic with a few essentials (a stainless-steel sink, standalone electric stove) and an expansive marble-topped antique table. The latter is outfitted with a spacious lower shelf to substitute for run-of-the-mill kitchen cabinets. Providing additional storage is a single open shelf, where the homeowner displays a collection of Swedish pottery.

A wall of 5 × 5-foot windows brings unobstructed views of the Catskill Mountains. Enhancing the natural light are walls and floors painted a barely-there shade of gray and plenty of white furniture like the pair of sofas and gold-trimmed armchair.

◄ The wall of windows continues to the dining area. To complement the jaw-dropping view, there's an unassuming mix of weather-worn antiques. Their rough-hewn look echoes the textures just outside.

➤ Tucking functional spots into otherwise unused nooks and crannies is a must with tiny-house living. Here, an American armchair, English sewing table, and Swedish mirror—all antiques—make a picturesque place to check e-mail or curl up with a book.

The open loft didn't allow for a proper guest room; however, a green Gustavian-era daybed is a dedicated spot for company to slumber. Exaggerating the coziness are green velvet bolster pillows.

The master bedroom skips a headboard in favor of the barn's handsome paneling. The bed is outfitted with simple Swedish linens and, to the right, features a handy lamp-cum-nightstand. Just beyond the bed, antique mirrors bring warmth and a sculptural element to the room.

▲ In lieu of a closet, the homeowner created a dressing nook with an oversize old mirror, a stool, hat boxes for storage, and an antique coat rack.

1 **Opt for a claw-foot tub.** As with many antiques, old claw-foot tubs tend to be smaller than modern-day offerings. This cast-iron example perfectly tucks into the bathroom. If the untouched look isn't your style, they can be reglazed for a nominal fee (usually around $100).

2 **Pull up a seat.** No, you may not sit for long stretches in a bathroom, but a perch like this one makes a pretty place for kicking off shoes, setting down toiletries, or stashing spare towels.

3 **Look for open vanities.** The leggy vanity style lends an airy feel to an otherwise cramped bathroom. If you need more storage, stash a few textured baskets below.

BIG IDEAS

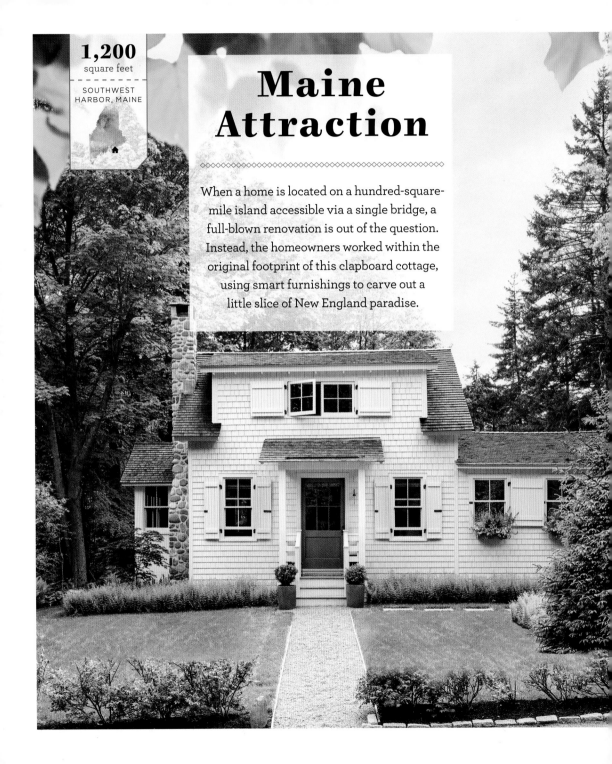

1,200
square feet

SOUTHWEST
HARBOR, MAINE

Maine Attraction

When a home is located on a hundred-square-mile island accessible via a single bridge, a full-blown renovation is out of the question. Instead, the homeowners worked within the original footprint of this clapboard cottage, using smart furnishings to carve out a little slice of New England paradise.

▲ Large roll arms can eat up floor space, which is why this sleek tuxedo-style sofa is perfect for a tiny space. Tufted detailing keeps the streamlined piece from feeling too modern in the country home. The combination of rattan and upholstery lends a collected look.

➤ On one side of the living room, the homeowners have an office by way of an old workbench outfitted with casters. (Easy to move in a pinch!) The rough-hewn desk has spacious drawers on either end, perfect for stashing laptop chargers and cords. Its rustic style also complements the reclaimed barn-wood hearth.

◄ With the kitchen's narrow layout, there wasn't room for a breakfast table *and* a prep island. Instead, an alternate plan was drawn up in the form of an antique drafting table. When it's not used as a spot for rolling dough or chopping vegetables, it's an inviting gathering spot, thanks to a trio of cowhide-covered stools.

The more wear there is over the years, the better the patina-loving finishes will look.

◄ In a space-starved kitchen, it's tempting to go the all-white route. But an eclectic mix of materials has a far warmer feel. This layered area features South Carolina barn wood (the cabinets and open shelves), galvanized metal (the countertops), soapstone (the sink), and even unlacquered brass (the hardware).

⌃ In a textbook example of work-with-what-you've-got, the homeowners converted a storage unit already on the property into the ultimate he-and-she shed. Now attached to the main house, it accommodates a queen-size bed flanked by custom floating bedside tables. Diminutive lamps and a homemade single-bulb pendant provide ample light without bulk, and a custom lumbar pillow, made from an Indian textile remnant, helps the room feel a bit wider.

▲ Yes, the guest room is tight (a mere ten feet wide), but what it lacks in square footage it makes up for in views, overlooking a scenic backyard filled with birch and spruce trees. The tiny table, which may be the world's smallest nightstand, is just big enough to accommodate a bud vase, mobile phone, or cup of coffee.

1 **Go all in with a dark hue.** Once a storage closet, the dining nook has a custom shade of charcoal on both the walls and ceiling. The enveloping look creates intimacy, not to mention a touch of drama.

2 **Bring on the built-ins.** A space-maximizing window seat allows the table to be placed close to the wall. For even more functionality, add a flip-top lid to the seats with piano hinges, carving out some unassuming storage for miscellaneous household items.

3 **Look for Lucite®.** Around the table, Lucite Danish-style chairs provide ample seating without eating up the visuals. The peekaboo material also makes for great barstools, coffee tables, and storage bins.

4 **Roll out a cowhide rug**. A traditional area rug might have overwhelmed the dining alcove, but a cowhide rug in a similar shade to the flooring brings subtle texture and plenty of floor protection. (Cowhides are designer favorites thanks to their easy-to-clean, can-take-a-beating surface.)

BIG IDEAS

1,200
square feet

VASHON ISLAND,
WASHINGTON

Logged In

Despite an extensive interior update,
the footprint of this historic log cabin—
the area's longest continually
inhabited structure—has remained
unchanged for 135 years.

To contrast with the raw wood paneling in the rest of the cabin, the dining room walls were coated with a soft whitewash. The brightened-up treatment helps the space—one of the tiniest in the house—feel much larger than it actually is. It also lets the reds and blues in the American flag create a patriotic pop.

▲ The handsome bedroom effortlessly
mixes old (a map of Vashon Island from the
1920s) with the new (a supple leather chair
from retailer J. Peterman). With storage at
a premium, oversize baskets, another new
purchase, were placed at the foot of the bed
for an eye-pleasing spot to stash bed linens.

➤ How do you complement a restored
cabin's raw wood? Outfit it with simple,
understated pieces that feel in keeping with
the historic structure. In the living room, for
example, four English engravings of farm
animals hang above a green mohair sofa.
Tree stumps turned into a coffee table bring
an outdoorsy element among the antiques.

A grouping of cow sketches pays homage to the locale and fills the vertical space without overshadowing the roughhewn paneling.

▲ A French armoire in the kitchen conceals retro-fitted pine shelves that house an impressive collection of white dinnerware, enamel cutlery, and antique linens.

1 **Take it outside.** What the cabin lacked in square footage is made up in acreage. Taking advantage of the latter, the homeowner implemented an alfresco dining spot for spring, summer, and autumn entertaining.

2 **Look for weather-resistant materials.** Outdoor furniture can turn shabby fast, which is why seeking out proper materials is a worthy investment. Here, a dining table made from Douglas fir (a type of wood that tends to resist decay, even when left unfinished) anchors the eating area.

3 **Grow an outdoor tapestry.** Scaling Boston ivy charts an unpredictable course along the side of an adjoining outbuilding. Whether you have a ho-hum surface or are limited on places to plop planters, a vertical garden adds an organic work of art.

BIG IDEAS

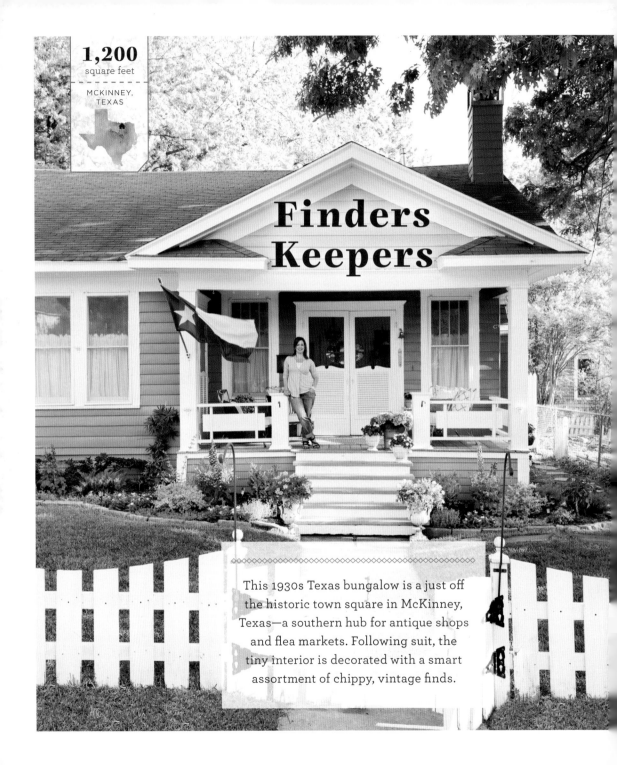

Finders Keepers

This 1930s Texas bungalow is a just off the historic town square in McKinney, Texas—a southern hub for antique shops and flea markets. Following suit, the tiny interior is decorated with a smart assortment of chippy, vintage finds.

The narrow living room called for strategic furniture placement. Cushy English roll-arm chairs were pushed up next to the fireplace and paired with swing-arm sconces and a trestle-style coffee table. And take note: Lurking amongst the shiplap above the fireplace are doors to a television cabinet.

In the dining room, a pine farmhouse table functions as both a work space and meal space, thanks to a duo of slipcovered armchairs. (Folding chairs are brought out when guests stop by.) A crystal chandelier and set of nautical prints help balance the room's more rough-hewn elements.

▲ A traditional headboard was skipped in favor of a twin bed tucked under a window. The bedding's sweet pink, red, and white color scheme makes a perfect foil to the rustic shiplap paneling.

▲ A proper master suite was created by transforming a five-foot-wide landing into a master bathroom—albeit a small one. Since a regular vanity wouldn't fit, a 1930s washstand was powder-coated white and fitted with a simple bowl sink. Thrift-store finds such as a wire shelf and enamel towel bar bring form and function to the room.

1 **Add a pop of black.** The dark hue will instantly ground a room, no matter the size. In this handsome kitchen, ebony-painted countertops are a pleasing midline focal point.

2 **Pour character into the sink.** This striking sink elevates the farmhouse style with an intricate brass detailing wrapped around the front.

3 **Make your dishwasher disappear.** Selecting a dishwasher the same color and profile as your kitchen cabinets will result in a less choppy, chaotic look. If a cabinet-fronted appliance isn't in the budget, consider replicating the look shown here. The white dishwasher is nearly invisible amongst the flat sailcloth panels lining the cabinet fronts.

4 **Keep lighting, well . . . light.** Pendant lights featuring cloth-covered cords and milk-glass shades not only hail from the era when the home was constructed; they also masterfully blend with the white walls.

BIG IDEAS

1,200
square feet

AUSTIN,
TEXAS

Open
Season

✕✕✕✕✕✕✕✕✕✕✕✕✕✕✕✕✕✕✕✕✕✕✕✕✕✕✕✕✕

The historic dogtrot-style home welcomes
with a classic exterior color combo of
black and white, plus a picturesque tree
swing. Inside, there's a put-it-on-display
aesthetic that brings heaps of personality.

▲ The homeowners put their kitchen walls to work with open shelves and hooks that make the most of the room's pitched ceiling. They also ditched the lower cabinets for more efficient freestanding components, including a stainless-steel rolling island and a mango-wood console topped with marble.

▲ A bank of moss-green built-ins lines one side of the kitchen, where an extensive collection of white service-ware pops against the verdant shade. With no cabinet doors in sight, the unconventional design creates a veritable art installation.

◄ What would have been a mere passageway becomes a full-fledged dining room with the introduction of a narrow 1840s tailor table, Windsor chairs, and forged iron chandeliers. High-gloss white paint, black trim, and curtain panels flanking the doorway further the effect.

➤ The living room lives large, thanks to nothing more than paint. There, high-gloss black walls bounce light from a pair of shutter-flanked windows. The bold shade also throws pale mid-century treasures (a Florence Knoll sofa and Arne Jacobsen egg chair) into sharp relief.

➤ No room for a full-size bed in a guest room? Ensure that a twin mattress is cozy with a snug daybed. The French blue one shown here has tall sides that allow for an extra-plush mattress and plenty of pillows. Complementing the antique sleeper is a darling dog portrait with its real-life subject lounging below.

▲ A little porch still deserves a big dose of style. Out back, French café chairs sit alongside a 1920s washtub that's planted with herbs; to the right, an espaliered magnolia tree functions as a living privacy screen.

1 **Instill calm with rich colors.** White may be the first thought for a tiny bedroom, but it doesn't have to be the only solution. Calm colors, like the master bedroom's taupe and muted teal, add depth that's at ease with the old paneling.

2 **Try a hanging light.** No space-sucking table lamp here! An inverted bell jar is paired with an Edison bulb and hung from the ceiling for an inventive reading light. It lends utilitarian panache to the rustic bedroom, and also alleviates the need for a bulky nightstand. Instead there's a diminutive chair stacked with books.

3 **Hang a black-and-white gallery wall.** The browns and sepia tones of old family photos pair well with the paint selections. Hung from the ceiling to nearly the floor, the oversize arrangement gives an illusion of height to the room.

Ranch Reform

This post-and-beam ranch-style house
gives new meaning to the term
"great room," with a hardworking
open floor plan that combines
living room, den, dining room, office,
and kitchen into a single space.

To help differentiate this lounging zone from the neighboring kitchen and den, the homeowners placed a mid-century leather sofa on a vintage shag rug. The floor-to-ceiling storage nook further divides the room and keeps books, blankets, and firewood at the ready.

Horizontal ticking stripes lend the appearance of width, as do the slats on the coffee table.

In the "great room's" second gathering area, it's all about scale. For example, hefty wingbacks would overpower the room and break up the visual flow, but the thirty-inch-tall barrel chairs are just right.

In this sunny nook, a banquette maximizes seating and storage. (The "built-ins" are simply kitchen cabinets, left over from the home's kitchen renovation, turned on their sides.) The inky-blue pillows echo the pops of indigo throughout the home, and the rattan pendant provides texture.

▲ The workspace squeezed in between the front door and refrigerator proves you can make any spot a functional one. The stainless steel wasn't particularly inspiring, so the homeowner dressed up the fridge with a barn-wood veneer. To help the desk blend in, it was painted the same shade of white as the walls.

1 **Decorate structural elements.** The kitchen's vaulted ceilings wouldn't be possible without sturdy (but unattractive) steel beams. For a prettier finish, they're wrapped in a nautical-inspired jute rope. The honey-hued tone is repeated in the room's light fixtures, island, and baskets.

2 **Make your island work overtime.** Tiny-house living can lead to irreverent storage. If you're able to incorporate a large island, don't limit it to kitchen supplies. This old workbench, for example, houses dry goods, office supplies, and even assorted wrapping papers.

3 **Hang "copy-cat" light fixtures.** Designers love to display contrasting light fixtures over an island and kitchen sink. But in a small cook space, a scaled-down version of the island pendants creates a more eye-pleasing and cohesive look.

4 **Add texture with penny tiles.** Large tiles are well and good; however, they can quickly overwhelm a size-starved kitchen (or bath, for that matter). Meanwhile, penny tiles paired with a matching grout bring a nubby aesthetic sans distraction.

BIG IDEAS

Hillside Hideaway

Rich color rules at this hillside hideaway.
Inside, navy blue covers the walls, creating
a cocoon-like feel; outside, a dusky gray-
green paint job coats every surface and
blends into the surrounding scenery.

In the living room, a round rattan coffee table, circular side table, and spherical floor lamp maximize space and soften the room's many hard edges (ceiling beams, paneled walls, stone fireplace).

Using saturated colors can make a tiny space feel intentionally jewelry box–like. While there are dark-blue walls throughout the home, that effect is best on display in the master bedroom. Here, the enveloping shade is matched with layered wool rugs underfoot. They provide much-needed insulation during frigid Pennsylvania winters.

▲ Reinforcing the blue's soothing vibe is the dark wood hutch. (The paneled backsplash is painted to give the illusion of a built-in cabinet.) Rummage-sale white dinnerware and a trio of blue Mason jars lend depth to the piece.

1 **Banish boundaries.** Taking inspiration from outside makes for a seamless indoors–outdoors transition and reinforces a sense of roominess. Two of the dining chairs, for example, are made from raw wood. A lush flower arrangement and fern-sprig centerpiece achieve a similar effect.

2 **Camouflage millwork.** Some old woodwork is striking, but that of DIY variety not so much. To conceal a hodgepodge of finishes and styles, go with a single all-encompassing color. A dark shade, like the blue shown here, is particularly helpful at masking past sins.

3 **Incorporate a barely-there piece.** Bring height to a room without visual heft with items such as this wire-and-glass plant stand. The inconspicuous find offers storage and subtle interest while letting the dining table remain center stage.

4 **Cast a filtered light.** A historic cabin begs for a bit of candlelight, but the old-world light source is rarely practical. You can achieve a similar ambience, and skip the fire hazard, with a chandelier sporting fabric shades. The petite canopies filter the light for an equally flattering glow.

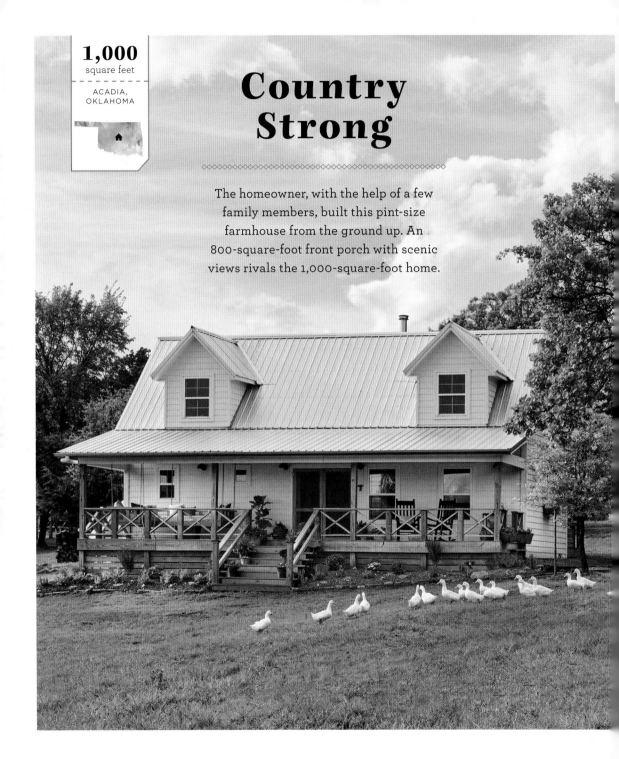

1,000
square feet

ACADIA,
OKLAHOMA

Country Strong

The homeowner, with the help of a few
family members, built this pint-size
farmhouse from the ground up. An
800-square-foot front porch with scenic
views rivals the 1,000-square-foot home.

Consider an energy-efficient wood-burning stove.

The small but open living room features shiplap paneling, wide-plank pine floors, and a trio of handsome built-in bookshelves, plus downsized furniture. Hiding among the classic country finishes are a few ingenious building materials, including stair railings crafted from cattle panels and a hearth with man-made rocks cast from stones from the Sierra Mountains.

The kitchen, the home's largest room, has custom cabinetry topped with black quartz countertops and complementary subway tile with black grout. The kitchen island serves as a dining spot for a family of four (when they're not eating on the porch) and is also the home for a built-in microwave and dishwasher. Above are IKEA pendants, disassembled and rewired with gas piping.

Feature a treasured family heirloom.

The lofted master bedroom provides a surprising amount of storage. Drawers beneath the bed and window seat hold the bulk of the homeowners' clothing. There's also workspace thanks to a petite antique desk paired with an old factory task light. Meanwhile, homemade floating shelves create a bedside perch. The windows were left bare to maximize the airy feel. The one exception: a vintage American flag that substitutes for a proper headboard.

▲ The well-feathered bath features a detailed gold mirror found at an estate sale. It pops off the dramatic royal-blue paint to make a statement.

1 Sneak in shallow shelves. Narrow shelving, especially in a kids' room, can house a wealth of treasures. Here, four-inch-deep ledges placed at the head and foot of the built-in bunk beds store artwork and toys, transforming them into display-worthy artifacts.

2 Look for industrial materials. In a tiny home, you can count on every last inch getting daily wear and tear. The black fitted pipe used to craft the bunk-bed ladder not only brings some utilitarian edge but is also hearty enough to withstand years of use.

3 Finish with a ray of sunshine. In a room with limited natural light, yellow accents, like these vibrant coverlets, can be a cheery substitute for the real thing. They pack an especially powerful punch in the tiny bunkroom.

BIG IDEAS

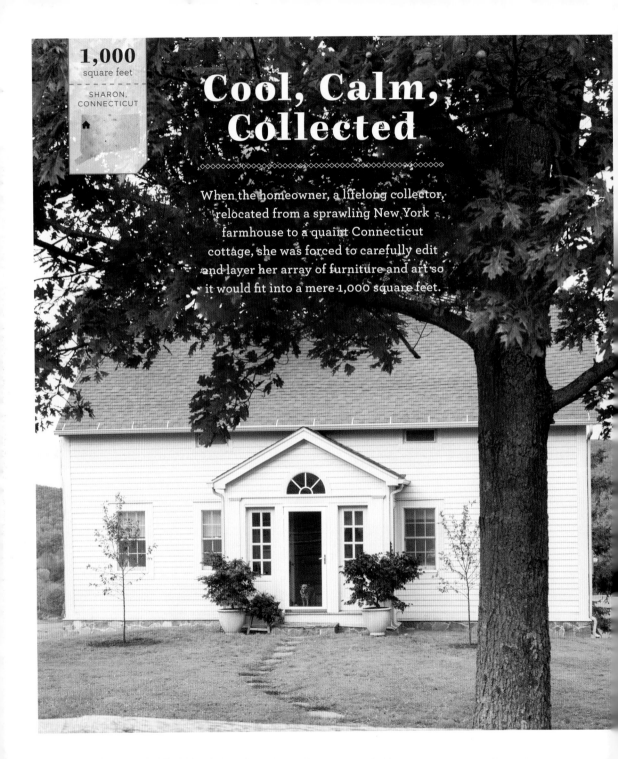

Cool, Calm, Collected

When the homeowner, a lifelong collector, relocated from a sprawling New York farmhouse to a quaint Connecticut cottage, she was forced to carefully edit and layer her array of furniture and art so it would fit into a mere 1,000 square feet.

A weathered blue trunk, which the homeowner has owned for more than thirty-five years, provides convenient and much-needed storage just inside the doorway. Other storage-lending antiques seen here include the zinc umbrella stand, faded apple basket, and ebony coat rack.

▼ The dining room is a mix of clean lines and vintage pieces. To make room for the antique hutch, a simple drop-leaf table was used in place of a larger, more formal piece. It's surrounded by Windsor chairs and a striped, flat-weave rug. Beyond, a circa 1880s ladder displays antique textiles that would have otherwise been hidden in a drawer.

➤ The hutch's vibrant mustard hue (original to the piece) introduces a bold accent color that reappears throughout the mostly neutral home.

The bedroom follows a simple formula: Start with neutral solids, then layer in select items with rich colors and intricate patterns. The latter come in the form of an Indian Kantha quilt, which was made from sari remnants, at the foot of the bed and a moody oil painting above.

▲ Building on the cottage's collected look are an assortment of black toleware trays displayed in a stunning arrangement in the living room. Encircling the largest one with other trays of varying scales creates a cohesive look among the mismatched patterns. Below, a weathered bench functions as a bookshelf that can be cleared off for seating in a pinch.

1 **Mute your palette.**
A monochromatic color scheme lets a kitchen feel larger than it actually is. Here the ceiling, walls, and cabinetry are all coated in a pale gray-green hue. For subtle dimension, the cabinets are painted 50 percent darker than the walls.

2 **Spring for built-in appliances.**
They may carry a heftier price tag, but built-ins like this cabinet-fronted dishwasher can be worth the investment in a tight kitchen. The discreet look helps the room appear unified.

3 **Embrace open cabinetry.**
Want to maximize space and add cottage style? Remove the doors from upper cabinets. The design trick brings a no-fuss vibe and increases a room's character by showing off treasured collections. More importantly, this style alleviates the aggravation that can come with opening cabinet doors in a cramped cook space.

4 **Roll out a runner.** A long, narrow rug instantly draws the eye in and generates the illusion of elongating the area. Here, the rich colors of a nineteenth-century Turkish runner lend a sophisticated anchor.

BIG IDEAS

In Bloom

Built in 1890, this quaint California
cottage was originally the gardener's
residence on a large estate. Today, flower-
filled landscaping remains, thanks to the
original occupant's green thumb.

The original floor is circa 1890.

The dining room's abundant natural light is maximized with mirrors. A reflective trio—two gilded, one bronze—amps up the sunshine and lets the area feel larger. Reinforcing the open feel are glass accents like the vases on the writing desk and the cloches atop the china hutch. The dark-stained floors—original to the home!—anchor the airy look.

▲ The walk-in pantry proves that nothing should go undecorated in a tiny home. Beadboard paneling and eye-pleasing open shelving take the utilitarian space from practical to downright pretty. Glass canisters and wicker bins keep (almost) everything in plain sight.

➤ Chandeliers, oil paintings, floor-length draperies, and an antique rug—in a kitchen? Yes! Dressing assures that the 100-square-foot room feels in keeping with the rest of the house.

◄ Rather than edit down a large collection of artwork, the homeowner made room for every cherished piece by creating a gallery wall that stretches from the crown molding to the baseboards. To the left of the display, a fresh mix of blue-and-white bedding keeps the room from feeling off-balance.

▲ A vibrant navy paint helps the 8 × 10-foot office feel cozy, not claustrophobic. Enhancing the homey feel are maps, flags, and a hodgepodge of nature paintings. Meanwhile, a cushy white slipcover sofa provides a visual break among the dark walls and accents.

▲ Doorways can throw a wrench in cramped spaces. To give this tiny *en suite* bath some breathing room, the homeowners replaced the existing hinged door with a red toile curtain panel. The textile improves traffic flow and also adds visual interest to the neutral bathroom.

1 **Add width with stripes.** A graphic black-and-white pattern adds punch to the narrow porch. While subtler color combos will also do the trick, you'll maximize elongation with a high-contrast duo like this one. Additional black accessories (planters, the iron settee) complement the floor motif.

2 **Embrace the structure.** Rather than attempting to camouflage a miscellany of architectural elements, let them happily coexist! Here window sashes, beadboard paneling, and shingled siding are left untouched and increase the porch's layered charm.

3 **Bring the indoors out.** Living room–worthy elements, like a blue dresser, velveteen seat cushion, and collage of hanging china, bring unexpectedly chic details outdoors. Pair them with a few outdoor essentials, like the rattan plant stand and galvanized planters, to help them look at home on a porch.

BIG IDEAS

880
square feet

NANTUCKET,
MASSACHUSETTS

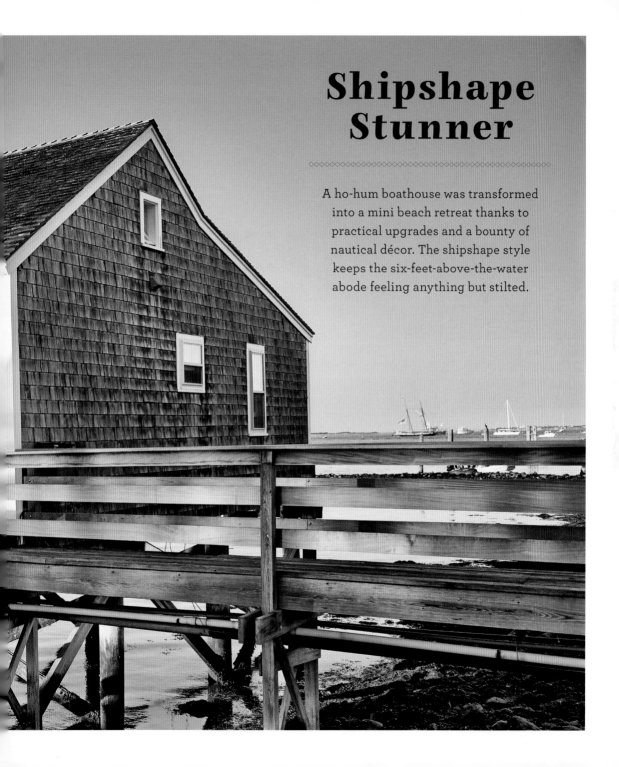

Shipshape Stunner

A ho-hum boathouse was transformed into a mini beach retreat thanks to practical upgrades and a bounty of nautical décor. The shipshape style keeps the six-feet-above-the-water abode feeling anything but stilted.

◄ While the 200-square-foot deck is far from roomy, the rolling two-tiered bar cart maximizes space—and mobility. Should a seaborne shower come through, the cart easily slides right back inside.

◄ Colorful sailing-race pennants, most of them from Cape Cod, draw the eye upward to showcase the fourteen-foot-tall ceilings. The homeowner left the wood-paneled ceiling unpainted to further exaggerate the height.

∧ The tiny window feels larger thanks to the paintings flanking it on either side. Their seascape motifs echo the vistas out the window, creating a more panoramic view than the single windowpane allows.

1 **Blur the interiors with the scenery.** Shades of blue (cotton duck upholstery) and tan (blinds, ceiling, table) mirror the sea and sand outside the boathouse. In a more landlocked locale, look to greens, browns, and grays to achieve a similar effect.

2 **Bridge the gap.** Matchstick blinds tie together the wood floors and ceilings and pop against the white tongue-and-groove walls. If a colorful paint job is more your thing, try a light fixture and rug in the same hue as the walls.

3 **Find foldable furniture.** Yes, it can be chic! White director chairs and a collapsible dining table look tiny in the eating nook but can rest flat against a wall to make room for gear storage in the off-season.

4 **Go big on personality.** In a limited space, use every chance to bring in character. Here, Nantucket-approved accents like an antique surfboard and old ship lights add heaps of visual interest. See also: the porthole on the blue front door (page 106).

BIG IDEAS

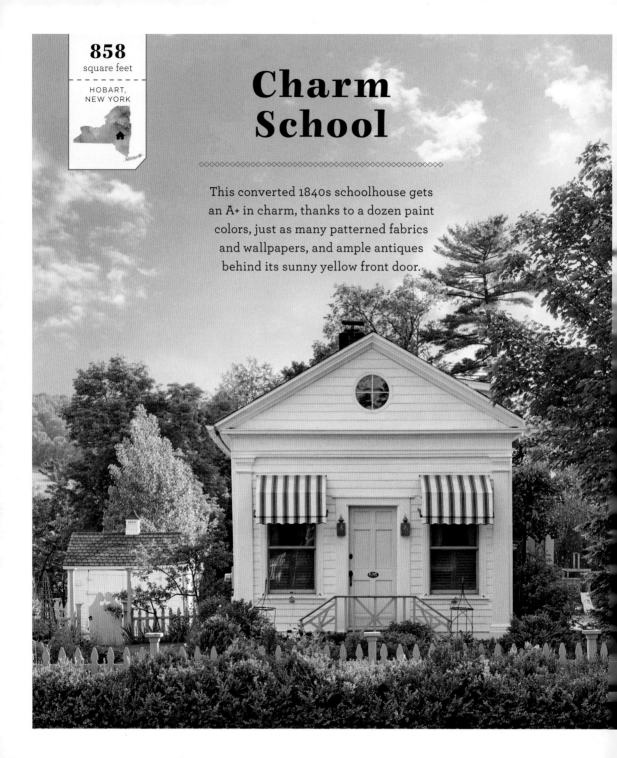

858
square feet

HOBART,
NEW YORK

Charm School

This converted 1840s schoolhouse gets
an A+ in charm, thanks to a dozen paint
colors, just as many patterned fabrics
and wallpapers, and ample antiques
behind its sunny yellow front door.

◄ With a limited number of walls to paint, the color-loving homeowners turned their attention to the ceiling in the living room, specifically the beams, which they coated in a vibrant shade of teal. Matching the intensity are bright yellow curtains and pink-drenched upholstery. The furniture's clean lines, particularly the tuxedo sofa, keep the large-scale fabrics from overpowering the narrow room.

⋀ The teal trim and yellow draperies continue into the dining space, which is anchored by a walnut dining table and an Asian-influenced secretary. The latter is where the homeowners stash their table linens and barware.

◄ In the low-pitched bedroom, every inch gets in on the act thanks to built-in bookshelves. The yellow shelving is the same as the cheery front door and coordinates with an accent color found on the room's floral wallpaper. Finally, a handsome oak bed contrasts the room's frill factor.

▲ As firm believers that there is no such thing as a pass-through space in a tiny cottage, the homeowners planted floral wallpaper up the stairwell. A high-gloss cream paint on the stair treads and trim helps to reflect the natural light, while framed artwork propped on a ledge infuses a collected air.

1 **Skirt the issue.** A skirted sink brings a softness to a bathroom's many hard edges and surfaces. It also provides an artful means of stashing less-than-eye-pleasing bathroom essentials: Hiding beneath this verdant and wonderfully intricate floral fabric are unsightly staples, such as toilet paper.

2 **Rethink the vanity mirror.** In this cramped bath, the only spot for the sink was right below the window. Rather than block the natural light source, mirrors were placed on either side of the vanity. The duo—one handheld, one on a retractable arm—works just as well as a single one would.

3 **Create a vertical garden.** While it's not a *real* vertical garden, floor-to-ceiling green can infuse calm. Here, a two-toned millwork-and-trellis wallpaper helps the bath take on a pastoral panache.

800
square feet

NAPA,
CALIFORNIA

One-Kit Wonder

This 22 × 24–foot kit barn sits on two acres in the heart of California wine country. The post-and-beam structure was constructed from hundreds of spruce planks that give the rustic escape just the right vintage.

◄ Circles abound in the designated dining area where a mirror, hats, and curvy chairs contrast the barn's many squared-off edges. But the most ingenious of the roundabout ideas is the dining table, which sits on large red casters, allowing the homeowner to roll the table outdoors when the weather is nice. (Spacious sliding barn doors make these a cinch!)

➤ In lieu of a full-fledged kitchen, the barn has a well-stocked island and this handsome bucket sink that's trimmed in blue and paired with exposed copper piping. Above, a two-by-four was placed between support beams for a rough-hewn dish ledge.

◄ In the kitchenette, salvaged wood and galvanized sheet metal from an 1880s barn are used on an island that functions as a bar on one side and a pantry on the other. Above, pendant lights crafted from chicken wire ramp up the rusticity and provide helpful task lighting.

⋏ The second floor is home to a lounging area where the star is a distressed-leather sofa. A plush plus-sign rug and handmade coffee table crafted from discarded shipping crates add to the sit-and-stay-a-while look.

⋏ In the bathroom, reclaimed lumber is a sturdy base for the concrete sink. To the left, a trough sourced from a feed-supply store is paired with a duck-cloth shower curtain for a barn-worthy spot to bathe.

➤ The nubby texture of the linen bed echoes the vibe of the barn walls. Topped with colorful bedding, including a vintage Pendleton blanket, it's an ideal spot for guests to hit the hay. The dapper green trunk at the foot of the bed handily stores extra bed linens.

1 **Supersize brackets.** Bracketed open shelving is in the domain of tiny kitchens. But the sturdy supports can also lend a hand with larger built-ins, like this spacious desk crafted from leftover plywood. The butted-against-the-wall design allows the piece of furniture to sit directly beneath the window. Below, the homeowners carved out a low-lying shelf.

2 **Catch some ZZZs.** Z-bracing, that is. The classic barn-door design adds country style. It will also keep exterior wooden doors from warping as the temperatures rise and drop.

3 **Cool down with concrete.** It's not uncommon for a tiny home to go without air conditioning. In this no-AC barn, poured concrete brings some chill factor to the flooring. The naturally cool material also stands up to muddy boots and dog paws and other frequent barn visitors.

BIG IDEAS

735
square feet

NEW YORK,
NEW YORK

City Savvy

◇◇◇◇◇◇◇◇◇◇◇◇◇◇◇◇◇◇◇◇◇◇◇◇◇◇◇◇◇◇

This tiny New York City dwelling brings
country flair to the big city with rough-
hewn collectibles set against neutral walls
and ample mirrors. In the dining room,
the homeowner's "display it, don't store
it" philosophy is showcased with linens
lining an old orchard ladder.

The rustic pitchforks make a down-home spot for hanging coats and scarves during the winter months.

CHANEL

▲ A cohesive color scheme makes for a curated, not cluttered, display.

◄ An unexpected assortment of humble finds, including ironstone platters and garden tools, brings sculptural interest to the narrow hallway.

◄ No above-the-sink view? No problem! This arched antique mirror maximizes the light that pours in nearby. It's one of fourteen mirrors (yes, fourteen!) that creates illuminating tricks of the eye throughout the apartment.

➤ Rooms with multiple purposes are essential in small-space living. In this living room, the homeowner used two twin beds to create a space-saving daybed large enough to accommodate the occasional overnight guest. An assortment of decorative pillows adds a cozy feeling when lounging at home.

▲ With drawers scarce, wares like clothespins and dog treats are on display in eye-pleasing glass canisters. The in-plain-sight theme continues above with staples scattered on the minimalist open shelves.

1 **Take a stand against traditional bedside tables.** You won't find ho-hum nightstands here. Instead, mismatched "tables" consist of a ghost chair and an old ballot box, the latter of which houses seasonal décor. Adding to unexpected storage is an old antique toolbox at the foot of the bed.

2 **Mix bucolic with urbane.** A tattered tobacco basket and sleek ghost chair are about as opposite as you can get with décor. But pairing juxtaposing items such as these brings instant interest. This particular combo brings depth to the cramped bedroom.

3 **Round up the right rug.** Bigger isn't always better. That's especially evident with this barely-two-foot (diameter) circular rug that rests beside the bed. After the homeowner exhaustively searched for a larger rectangular version, she honed in on the round jute floor covering. It's just the right size to greet feet first thing in the morning.

BIG IDEAS

700
square feet

MINNEAPOLIS,
MINNESOTA

Lofty Aspirations

This downtown Minneapolis loft is part of a rehabbed circa-1880s factory. It features tall ceilings and oak-planked floors. To play up its historic architecture and urban locale, the homeowner mixed farmhouse-worthy pieces, such as a rolling island topped with packing-crate slats, with industrial elements like the metal barstools.

◄ The loft's unusual, angled recess (it conceals an air vent) was no match for the clever homeowner, who lined it with spruce shelving to hold a treasured book collection. Below is an enclosed portion of the air-conditioning unit, which serves as a side table. The antique doll chair resting on top feels right at home in the tiny space.

➤ Simple utilitarian style is the name of the game in the kitchen, where open shelves display handmade pottery and Swedish cleaning brushes. An unassuming over-mount sink and easy-to-clean laminate countertops reinforce the minimalist aesthetic.

Proof that less can truly be more—a dining area is carved out by the front door with the help of four folding bistro chairs and a hand-me-down table. A textured linen tablecloth lends a bit of sophistication.

Ingenuity abounds in the bathroom. A vintage chest full of towels rests beneath an antique table that provides a generous surface area for makeup and other necessities. (There's even room for a potted plant!) Equally hardworking are the old-school medicine cabinet and wooden ledge above the sink.

Clover-printed shams and a duvet cover are the focal point in the bedroom, where an antique canopy bed brings an architectural element to the plain-Jane interiors.

1 **Double up on daybeds.** Fitted with twin mattresses, a duo of daybeds (deeper than a love seat but not as long as a full sofa) brings a French-salon vibe to the living room. The seating can also easily transition to a guest room.

2 **Layer rugs.** And then layer some more. A wide-open floorplan is an efficient setup for a tiny home. But it can make rug placement tricky—and expensive! For an alternative to a single sprawling floor covering, try overlapping flat-weave indoor/outdoor rugs. There are no fewer than ten in this inviting living room.

3 **Leave windows bare.** The loft's skinny-dipping windows mean zero obstruction to the natural light. Adding to the au naturel appeal, the original window sashes were left unpainted to generate some rustic texture against the glossy white walls.

BIG IDEAS

665
square feet

DAYTON,
WYOMING

Use trim to finish.

Forest Station

This tiny cabin, nestled in the Wyoming mountains, was built *and* furnished on a shoestring budget. Its shrewd homeowner proved a master at tiny-house tricks and frugal finds. In the living room, the white bookcases look like custom built-ins but are from a big-box retailer. The white sofa is upholstered with paint dropcloths, and the striking red club chair came from a thrift store.

▲ The kids' lofted bedroom features homemade platform beds with pullout drawers below. The cleverest trick? The homeowner fashioned three sets of sheets to perfectly fit the custom beds out of a single on-sale, king-size set.

◄ With country elements—beadboard paneling, ladderback chairs—the dining nook looks like it belongs in a sprawling old farmhouse. But the charming new eating area only takes up a nominal portion of the open-floorplan home thanks to a space-saving window seat and narrow antique table.

▲ In the master bedroom, slim wardrobes with inset ledges take the place of beside tables. Above the bed, an oval mirror—another thrift-store find!—acts as the room's second window, opening up the 8 × 13–foot space.

1 **Fake it on countertops.** These "soapstone" counters are actually plywood, coated in chalkboard paint and sealed with paste wax. If you prefer the look of marble, you can pull off a similar DIY with subtly swirled paint.

2 **Join the draft.** No space-hogging hood here! Instead a Jenn-Air® downdraft range frees up walls and still keeps air circulating—an important task in a cramped kitchen.

3 **Do some eavesdropping.** What makes this kitchen so striking? It's arguably the sunshine-filled window tucked in below the eaves. Little cook spaces are often starved for natural light; sneaking windows into unexpected spots such the rafters or even ceiling can do wonders to open them up.

BIG IDEAS

Party On

This 30 × 30–foot barn was designed with entertaining in mind. Equipped with an efficiency kitchen, sleeping loft, and even a stage, it's primed for parties that last well-into-the-night. (Or even all weekend long.) Hefty hemlock beams and fiery red barn doors add to the festive feel.

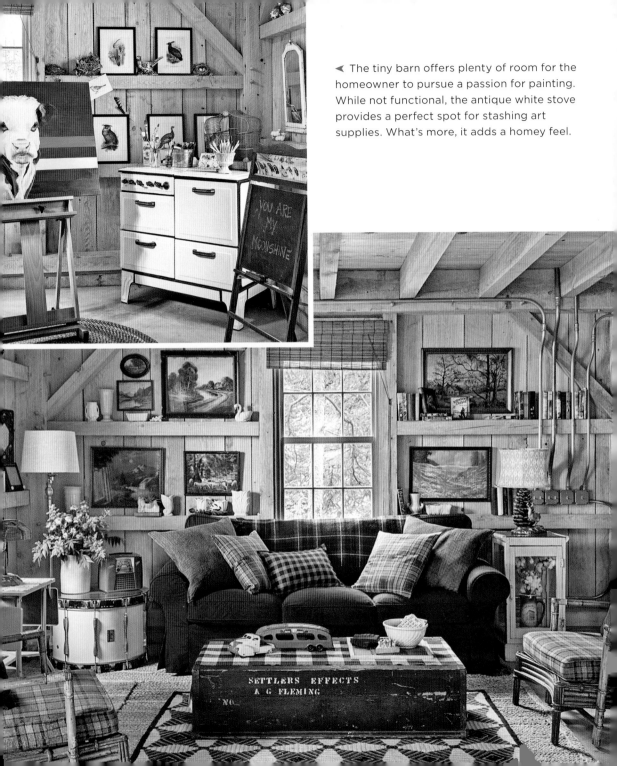

◄ The tiny barn offers plenty of room for the homeowner to pursue a passion for painting. While not functional, the antique white stove provides a perfect spot for stashing art supplies. What's more, it adds a homey feel.

◄ The homeowner's décor motto: Barn outside; camp inside. The latter is in full effect in the living area, where a red sofa is surrounded by plenty of plaid and paint-by-numbers. Taking advantage of the shelf-like beams formed by the timber frame, the homeowner adds to the lodge feel with displays of yellow ware and vintage board games.

▲ The best seat in the house? The wooden bench and metal Tolix® chairs gathered around the large antique table. Beyond, there's a would-be stage where the homeowner hosts impromptu concerts.

⋀ Even when not teeming with guests, the barn is packed with "characters" by way of numerous vintage collectibles. Vibrant retro thermoses quench the thirst for color among the structure's many wood tones.

➤ The quaint sleeping loft contains an inviting twin bed complete with wool blankets and a quirky pillow sporting Theodore Roosevelt's likeness. Beside the bed, the homeowner carved a nightstand from the stump of a dying tree removed during the barn's construction.

1   Tuck and go. Under-the-gables spaces are the domain of tiny houses. This one makes the most of the cramped loft with low-profile furniture, including a compact bed (there's no headboard!) and a shallow trunk and short crate in lieu of a traditional dresser and nightstand.

2   Sneak in storage. The minimalist bedroom stealthily houses spacious pullout drawers that provide much needed storage without comprising floorspace or headroom.

3   Walk the line. The stripes on a vintage wool coverlet tuck in bold pops of color. More importantly, they help the narrow loft space feel wider than it actually is. A plaid throw blanket and checked pillow create a similar visual effect.

BIG IDEAS

600
square feet

DOUGLAS,
GEORGIA

Garden Variety

This is more than a greenhouse. Outfitted with interior niceties like sofas and area rugs, it's a garden retreat with a jewel-box feel. The abode features 139 salvaged windows, all sporting a coat of teal paint that achieves the unthinkable: It both blends in with and stands its own against the verdant surroundings.

▲ What's a garden house without a little gardening? Potted flowers in mossy containers are mixed with a sculptural display of gardening trinkets for an earthy, eye-pleasing vignette.

◀ Decorating an outdoor structure calls for materials that can take a beating. Here, gardening tools-turned-artwork like the pitchfork, shovel, and shears are mounted to a cast-off French door. Below it's equipped with a mirror to further reflect the lush view.

▲ A weathered green bistro table and chairs echo the house's signature hue and also beg for someone to sit and enjoy a spot of tea. Just behind the table, a stunning collection of antique oil lamps is nestled in wire garden baskets and will amp up the ambience at sundown.

1 **Cage it in.** Indoors or out, an antique bird cage is an alluring way to introduce architectural interest and plenty of storage. The oversize one shown here is a pretty place to conceal gardening essentials, such as potting soil and gloves.

2 **Raise a (transparent) roof.** Yes, this garden house wows with nearly 150 windows, but it also features clear corrugated plastic roof panels that let light stream in from above. The hardy, affordable material can hold its own against the inevitable elements.

3 **Wow with wicker.** Real-deal, old-fashioned wicker has a ladylike air about it. But don't let that fool you—it was built to last. Incorporating wicker into an almost-alfresco space like this one is a foolproof way to bring living room elegance outside.

BIG IDEAS

500
square feet

ELKINS,
NEW HAMPSHIRE

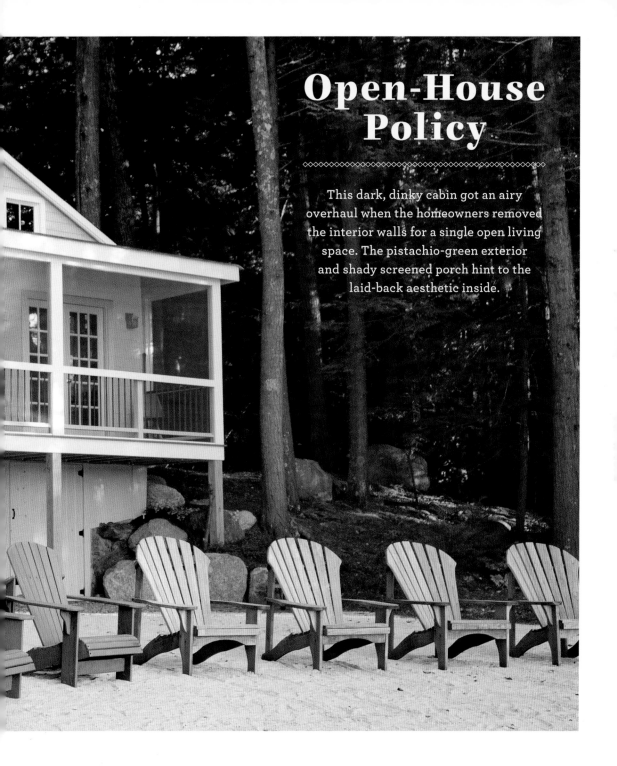

Open-House Policy

This dark, dinky cabin got an airy overhaul when the homeowners removed the interior walls for a single open living space. The pistachio-green exterior and shady screened porch hint to the laid-back aesthetic inside.

▲ The cabin is equipped with dozens of outdoor pieces that can stand up to muddy feet and wet bathing suits. For example, the wicker sectional was actually designed for a patio. Same goes for the striped area rug. Also in abundance: cubbies. Whether built-in or repurposed antiques, the cabin has spots to stash items like beach blankets and sunscreen at every turn.

➤ Since the kitchen is part of the main living area, it needs to look good. Handsome selections like a porcelain sink atop a unique accordion table and a fridge dressed up with maps do the trick. Quintessential lake-cabin accents like duck decoys add further charm to the smart gray shelving.

The renovation wiped out the cramped bedrooms in favor of more living space. But the homeowners still managed to tuck a quaint sleeping loft into the rafters. Resting on the floor are two single futon mattresses wearing vintage wool and alpaca throw pillows. Old highway maps tacked to the wall form makeshift headboards and give a shout-out to the homeowner's state pride.

▲ The cabin's bathroom is cramped, but its outdoor shower feels wonderfully spacious, thanks to a shuttered window that provides shoreline views. The exterior's pale green hue reinforces the one-with-nature sensation of the space.

1 **Use it or lose it.** Realizing sit-down dinners are virtually nonexistent at their lake escape, the homeowners nixed a proper dining area. In its place, they wheeled in a crowd-pleasing bar cart with plenty of room for pouring cocktails and stashing table linens.

2 **Roll with it.** Everything is better on wheels when it comes to tiny-home living. Case in point: Oversize casters let the bar cart transition to al fresco entertaining or be moved out of the way altogether if more seating is required.

3 **Keep gear in plain sight.** Rather than trying to cram it into one of the home's few closets, the homeowners let lake gear like fishing nets and canoe paddles stand in for artwork. The sporting look also works with tennis rackets, golf clubs, and more.

BIG IDEAS

LIVE FREE OR DIE
GH 5C82

480
square feet

HARPERSVILLE,
ALABAMA

Work of Art

This garden retreat proves a little house can make a big entrance with double doors painted a daring shade of teal. Hinged windows along both the top and bottom provide lovely cross breezes day and night, making the structure is inviting inside as it is out.

➤ The sunny art studio inspires plenty of creative repurposing ideas, including an antique table-turned-desk, music stand-turned-art easel, and feed trough-turned-storage bins. Equally imaginative: stashing books among the rafters.

◄ Terra-cotta pots become a veritable art installation, thanks to custom shelves set against the reclaimed windows. Touches like a desk lamp further infuse homey style.

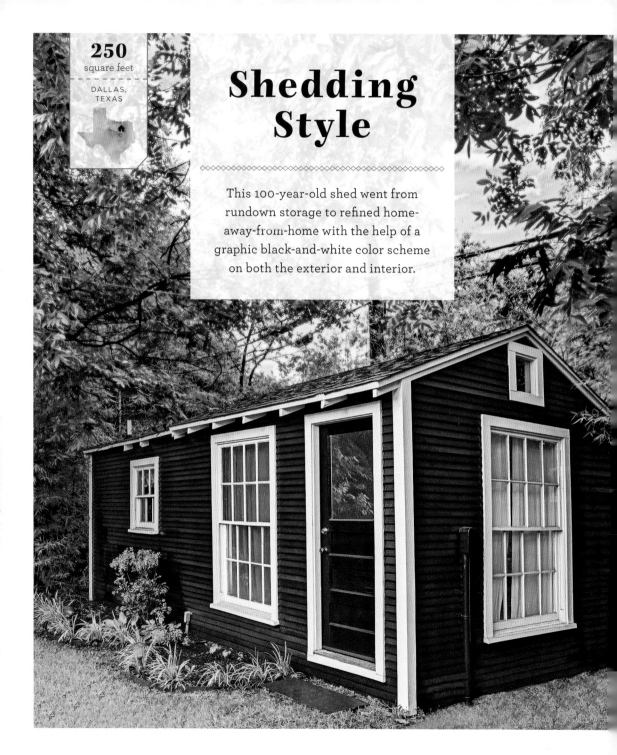

250
square feet

DALLAS,
TEXAS

Shedding
Style

This 100-year-old shed went from
rundown storage to refined home-
away-from-home with the help of a
graphic black-and-white color scheme
on both the exterior and interior.

The "living room" feels cozy not only because of its size, but also thanks to the many textured elements including throw blankets, a shell chandelier, and a fiddle leaf fig tree.

◄ An understated palette of black and white doesn't overwhelm the modest kitchen, where a mini-fridge stands in for a standard-size one. The homeowner constructed a frame around the pint-size appliance to give the little cook space a more polished look.

➤ For stealth storage in the bathroom, the homeowner used Velcro® to secure a ticking stripe skirt to the sink, which was uncovered below the floorboards during the shed renovation. A pair of curvy mirrors creates the illusion of more room, and a simple arrangement of book pages adds an artful touch.

▲ A thematic grouping of art—here, mid-century female portraits—keeps a gallery wall feeling cohesive, not chaotic. Their traditional forms also balance more eccentric pieces, like the spire mirror and face-adorned ceramic vase.

1 **Be one with nature.** Having natural elements indoors—herbs, houseplants, even a branch as a "rod"—helps the interior feel like an extension of the yard.

2 **Make walls work overtime.** Tiny-house living calls for using as much vertical space as possible, whether it's a rafter-skimming ladder displaying blankets, like the one shown here, or open shelving to keep items at arm's reach.

3 **When in doubt, add stripes.** Stripes widen and elongate, which is why the homeowner used them on a black-and-white rug, which helps establish a teeny "foyer" in the shed.

BIG IDEAS

192
square feet

NATCHEZ,
MISSISSIPPI

Southern Comfort

A working Mississippi farm welcomes a stylish newcomer by way of a baby-blue "she-shed." The barn-inspired structure has living-room details that make it the perfect spot to while away an afternoon.

◄ Summer afternoons were made for napping. With that in mind, a metal daybed offers ample room for curling up without encroaching on floor space. Above, a hand-tufted mattress in classic ticking stripe provides a second spot for shed visitors to catch some shuteye. For water-resistant flooring, a click-and-lock vinyl tile was applied over the subflooring. Finally, an oversize vintage American flag sets a festive tone for the backyard retreat.

➤ To equip for entertaining, there's a kitchenette with a mini-fridge and an assortment of whitewashed wooden crates stocked with pantry and party staples. Above, thin sheets of metal (affixed to plywood using spray adhesive) provide a sleek magnetic surface to tack up pictures and postcards.

▲ An entry nook takes shape by the front door, where a collection of grab-and-go sunhats adds texture to the room. Below, a galvanized bin keeps easy-to-misplace items close at hand. Vintage finds like license plates and baskets reinforce the casual vibe.

1 **Add architectural extras.** To help the structure feel less "shed" and more "retreat," the straight-from-mail-order tool shed was outfitted with slated shutters. And because country thunderstorms sound better against a metal roof, a galvanized one was added.

2 **Take a firewood rack up a notch.** Lay a chunky piece of plywood across the top of a metal firewood rack and— ta-da!—you have an outdoor bar ready for in-the-field entertaining.

3 **Match the paint to the surroundings.** The originally brown shed got a country upgrade with blue and green paint on the exterior, which mimic rolling fields and expansive skies.

BIG IDEAS

Small Wonder

This mobile farmhouse offers up ample functions and top-of-the-line finishes, like hardwood floors, aged-bronze sconces, and a happy yellow front door that's only twenty-nine inches wide. The best part? Because it is built on wheels and classified as a travel trailer, the owners can take this stylish show on the road and park it almost anywhere.

⋀ In the two-foot-wide niche above the toilet, custom floating shelves corral toiletries and belie the home's prefab origins.

◀ A narrow sink basin makes way for a shower insert that features a high-pressure, low-flow showerhead—a spa-like experience scaled down to just four square feet.

◀ Just inside the front door is a living area complete with a pair of comfy chairs. Above, a lofted shelf, accessible by a stowaway ladder, provides six square feet of storage for bulky items like suitcases and out-of-season clothes.

◄ Talk about cozy: This four-foot-high loft (that's at its peak!) is just wide enough to fit a king-size bed. The same white tongue-and-groove paneling used throughout the home, plus four awning-style windows and a skylight, help the snug space feel roomier.

▼ No need for this travel trailer to hit up a laundromat. A washer/drier combo unit fits inside the two-foot-wide closet, which has an additional four feet of storage squeezed in above.

1 **Spice it up.** Well-thought-out storage is obligatory in a house this tiny. This two-inch-deep shelf is perfectly sized to keep cooking spices handy.

2 **Warm up to a nautical idea.** Little mobile homes have a lot in common with houseboats. Here, a made-for-a-marine-vessel propane heater keeps the entire home toasty during the winter months.

3 **Scale down subway tile.** The simple glazed design is a classic for a reason. To make it work in a teeny kitchen, look to a petite variety, like this 1.5 × 3–inch version.

BIG IDEAS

Happy Little Camper

From the custom exterior paint job to the hardwood flooring, this 1973 vintage camper—affectionately known as "The Nugget"—is a personality-filled home away from home.

Wherever it makes a pit stop, the itty-bitty camper greets company with an Instagram®-ready door mat. Adding to the homey feel is a retro-inspired wooden door. With five narrow glass panes and a honey-hued tone, it's far more inviting than the original aluminum one.

The homeowner powder-coated the stove top with a bold melon paint, turning the practical appliance into a funky focal point. White cabinets and a high-gloss penny-tile backsplash let the color pop.

The table drops down to allow space for a bed.

Believe it or not, this whimsical corner can transition into sleeping quarters. Day or night, the asymmetric brass chandelier brings a warm, sculptural glow.

1 **Use neutrals for balance.** In a trailer this size, you see *everything* the moment you walk in. To infuse color but avoid a disorienting rainbow effect, try to select accent colors (a mix of sherbet hues does the trick here), and stick to whites and grays for the rest.

2 **Cultivate road-proof plants.** To make sure greenery stays upright in transit, the homeowners built a shelf with individual holes for potted plants.

3 **Roll with it.** Even a travel trailer needs some privacy. For window treatments that take up almost zero space, look to a roll-up variety, like the white linen ones sported by "The Nugget." Handsome leather straps hold them in place when not in use.

Room with a View

What this tree house lacks in right angles (zero!) and square footage, it more than makes up for in natural light and evening breezes. That's due, in large part, to a hodgepodge of old windows that were the guiding light in the quirky design.

Mid-century pieces like the rattan sofa and groovy floor lamp balance the treehouse's rustic style. The juxtaposition ensures that the escape feels decidedly grown-up. Bringing a fresh pop of color to the room is a bright blue trunk that functions as a coffee table and also conceals cleaning supplies.

The ten-inch-wide wood slabs on antique brackets add charm and keep odds and ends at arm's reach. Of particular note, the copper kettle resting on a hot plate provides piping-hot cups of post-nap tea.

A diminutive oak secretary is so pretty that you *almost* don't notice the floor-to-ceiling tree views just beyond it. Plants and branches plucked from the neighboring garden make the retreat feel even more at one with nature.

1 **Build around the bed.** No sleeping bags for this treehouse. Instead, the homeowners designed the entire treehouse around this antique iron bed. Doing so assured that the structure could function as a proper guest house in addition to a backyard hangout.

2 **Branch out with textiles.** Aptly named bark cloth makes an appearance on the bed by way of floral pillows. The nubby fabric, so called for its wood grain–like appearance, was popular in the 1950s and '60s. Today it's an affordable way to incorporate texture into a tiny home.

3 **Utilize duct work.** Space-zapping duct work gets a pass this time due to the shallow built-in shelf—a perfect treehouse nightstand. Its boxy shape is mimicked by the floral canvas hanging above.

PHOTO CREDITS

Cover photography © David Hillegas: front;
© Victoria Pearson: back

© Matt Albiani: 106–107, 108, 109, 110–111

© Lucas Allen: 5 right

© Jean Allsopp: 15, 16 right

© Mali Azima: 17

© James Baigrie: 14

© Lincoln Barbour: 10 left

© Stacey Brandford: 36, 37, 38–39, 39 right, 40–41

© Roger Davies: 99, 100, 101, 102, 103, 104 left, 104–105

© Erica George Dines: 152, 153, 154 left, 154–155

© Tara Donne: 11

© John Gruen: 92, 93, 94, 95, 96 left, 96–97

© Mandi Gubler: 184–185, 186, 187, 188–189

© Audrey Hall: 120, 121, 122, 123, 124, 125, 126–127

© Alec Hemer: 70, 71, 72, 73, 74 left, 74–75

© David Hillegas: 7, 190–191, 192, 193, 194–195

iStockphoto: © Creative_Improv: chapter openers
(watercolor swatch), © miniature: chapter openers (states),
© Robin Olimb: chapter openers (Alberta)

© Max Kim-Bee: i, viii, 29, 16 left, 28, 30, 31, 32, 33, 34 left,
34–35, 52, 53, 54, 55, 56 left, 56–57, 98, 112, 113, 114 left,
114–115, 116, 117, 118 left, 118–119, 156–157, 158, 159, 160–161, 162
left, 162–163

© David A. Land: ii–iii, 8, 20, 22 left, 22–23, 24, 25, 26 left,
26–27

© Randy Mayor: 4

© Helen Norman: 18–19, 144–145, 146, 147, 148 left, 148–149,
150–151

© Victoria Pearson: 5 left, 76–77, 78, 79, 80 left, 80–81, 140,
141, 142 left, 142–143

© Ian Pratt: 176–177, 178, 179, 180–181, 181 right, 182–183

© Armando Rafael: 82, 83, 84 left, 84–85

© Lisa Romerein: 58, 59, 60, 61, 62 left, 62–63, 134, 135, 136,
137, 138–139

© Annie Schlechter: 42–43, 44–45, 46, 47, 48, 49, 50 left,
50–51, 86, 87, 88, 89, 90 left, 90–91

© Buff Strickland: 2–3, 65, 64, 66, 67, 68–69

© Cody Ulrich: 166, 167, 168–169, 169 right, 170 left, 170–171

© Bjorn Wallander: 13 right

Courtesy West Elm: 6 left

© Brian Woodcock: 6 right, 10 right, 12, 13 left, 128, 129, 130
left, 130–131, 132 left, 132–133, 164, 165, 172, 173, 174 left,
174–175

INDEX

HEARSTBOOKS

An Imprint of Sterling Publishing Co., Inc.
1166 Avenue of the Americas
New York, NY 10036

ISBN 978-1-61837-254-3

Distributed in Canada by Sterling Publishing
c/o Canadian Manda Group, 664 Annette Street
Toronto, Ontario M6S 2C8, Canada
Distributed in Australia by NewSouth Books
45 Beach Street, Coogee, NSW 2034, Australia

For information about custom editions, special
sales, and premium and corporate purchases, please
contact Sterling Special Sales at 800-805-5489 or
specialsales@sterlingpublishing.com.

Manufactured in China

2 4 6 8 10 9 7 5 3 1

sterlingpublishing.com
countryliving.com

Cover design by Jo Obarowski
Book design by Shubhani Sarkar
Photography credits on page 196